The book about kitties

by Mary Celeste Deck

PRICE/STERN/SLOAN
Publishers, Inc., Los Angeles
1978

Mary Celeste Deck wrote and illustrated her book about kitties when she was a seven year old second grader in Santa Cruz, California.

Copyright © 1978 by Mary Celeste Deck
Published by Price/Stern/Sloan Publishers, Inc.
410 North La Cienega Boulevard, Los Angeles, California 90048.
Printed in the United States of America. All rights reserved.

ISBN: 0-8431-0457-0

When a cat sters at you he wants to Play ball.

When a cats legs
get short that means
he sees a bird. don't
let him get it.

It wont be fun to play in yore sand-box if yore cat dosnt haf a litter-box.

Cats like to sit on visiters laps, espeshily if they dont like cats.

If you wake up and hear a baby cring out-side it mite be yore cat.

If you dont like the feel of sand-paper then dont let yore cat licke you,

When a cat puts it's Paws on you he wants to be held. Hold him!

If you leve butter out on the tabel the next day you will have a fat cat.

Somtimes yore cat
will try to catch a
fly. dont let him do
it cuz its yekky if
he eats it.

When he claws the
curtains don't let him
do it. get a clawer
for him.

curtains

you will not hafto give
yore cat a bath cuz
he alredy know's how
to cleen himself. dogs
dont.

Never let any kind of
meet thaw out where
yore cat mite be abel
to get it or else you
will get in big troble.

meet
↙

Snail bate woud kill yore cat if he ate it. Dont let him eat it!

The best thing too do
is put beer out for

the snails. If yore cat
drinks the beer he prablie
woud'nt like it.

If a cat wants
to be alone, he
runs away you leve
him alone!

When a cat is sleepy, he always cleans himself then gose to sleep always.

If you find feathers on the porch see what yore cat has been up to.

When a kittie looks up at the air for a long time that means its getting reddy to jump.

If yore nayber hates cats keep yore cat out of sight of the nayber or they will go crazey.

If yore riding in a car with yore cat, keep the windows rold up or else hill jump out.

If yore gramma has pantyhose on, dont let yore cat claw her or gramma will screem.

If you li've neer a free-way its best to keep yore cat indors. for a outdore cat mite get run over.

.

If you dont want furr
all over yore black dress
then dont let yore
cat sit on you.

Put yore cat out of sight of little kids cuz they anooy cats.

If you find one of yore indoor plants has been duggin up, dont worry it was prablie yore cat who used the bathroom.

When a cat sees a dog, it's furr fluffs up and it's tail goes up, you hafto save yore cat.

Set traps for gofers
so the cat dosnt bring
them in the house
and scare the baby
sitter.

If you think yore cat is lost lisen for funny noises in cubrards and walls. I think you mite find him.

When you want to get
yore cat out from under
a bed just shake his
food box and say kitty
kitty and hill come.

When a cat has to go to the bathroom he jumps on you. You let him out!

If you have a girl cat don't get it spaid so it can have kittens!

If yore cat gets fat, get reddy for a big saprize.

kittens!

Yore cat mite not like the place you piked out for it to have its babys.

If you have a wite girl
cat and a black boy cat
this is what the kittens
will look like.

If you want to pik
up kittens pik them
up by the skruf of
the nek.

Kittens dont need
flee kollers cuz there
mother cleens them
alreddy.

If you have a fish
put it some place
ware the cat cant get
it.

If you have lots of mice in yore house you bedder put a bell aroun yore cats nek or else yore house will be a big mess from mice.

pss!

PRICE/STERN/SLOAN
Publishers, Inc., Los Angeles